About This Book

Title: *Can You Spot the Spots?*

Step: 2

Word Count: 121

Skills in Focus: S-blends

Tricky Words: small, sea, fish, farm, jungle, bird, animals, hide, kinds

Ideas For Using This Book

Before Reading:
- **Comprehension:** Look at the title and cover image together. Walk through the pictures in the book with readers and have them make predictions about what they might learn in the book. Help them make connections by asking what they already know about animals with spots.
- **Accuracy:** Practice saying the tricky words listed on page 1.
- **Phonemic Awareness:** Explain to readers that a blend is two consonants together that each make a sound. Discuss that some blends include the letter *s*. Read aloud story words containing s-blends, beginning with *spots*. Segment the sounds in the word slowly and have the students call out the word. Call attention to each blend and where it is found within the word. More s-blend story words include *sniffs*, *stands*, *must*, *smell*, *swim*, *slips*, *past*, and *nest*.

During Reading:
- Have readers point under each word as they read it.
- **Decoding:** If readers are stuck on a word, help them say each sound and blend the sounds together smoothly. You may want to point out s-blends as they appear.
- **Comprehension:** Invite students to talk about what new things they are learning about spotted animals while reading. What are they learning that they didn't know before?

After Reading:
Discuss the book. Some ideas for questions:
- What spotted animals have you seen?
- Why do you think some animals have spots?

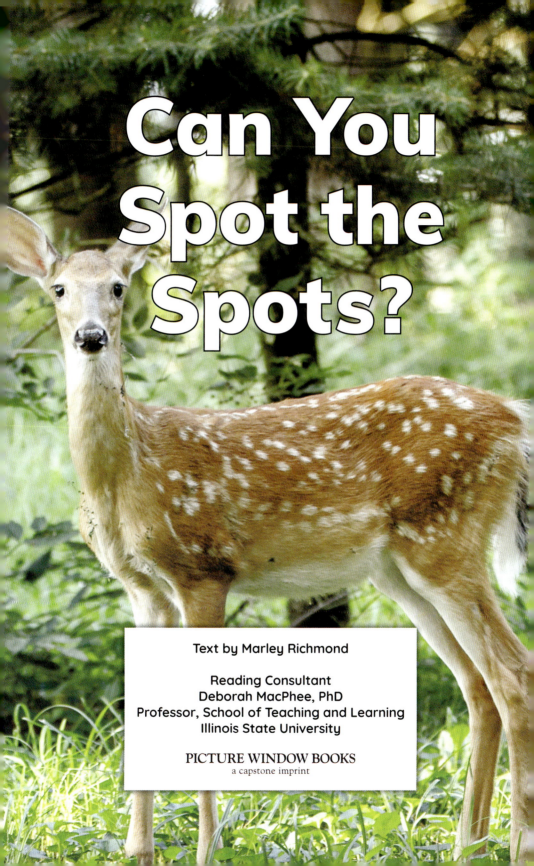

Can You Spot the Spots?

Text by Marley Richmond

Reading Consultant
Deborah MacPhee, PhD
Professor, School of Teaching and Learning
Illinois State University

PICTURE WINDOW BOOKS
a capstone imprint

The man has a dog.
It has lots of small spots.

His dog sniffs and sniffs.

Can you spot the spots in the sea?

Kids swim in the sea. A fish slips past.

Fish with spots can blend in.

Can you spot the spots on farms?

Cows have big spots.
Lots of cow spots
are black.

A pig has spots.
It has spots on its skin.

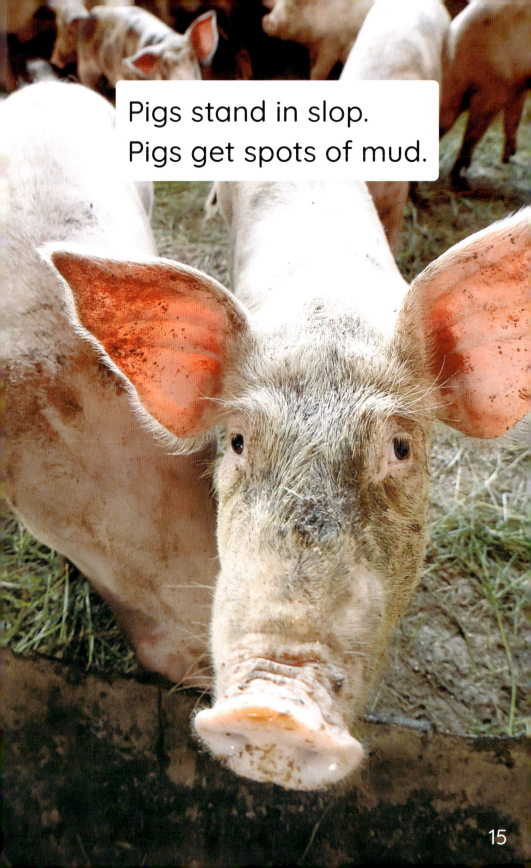

Pigs stand in slop.
Pigs get spots of mud.

Can you spot the spots in the jungle?

Frogs have spots.
Their spots can be black.

Big cats have spots.

Spots help big cats hide.

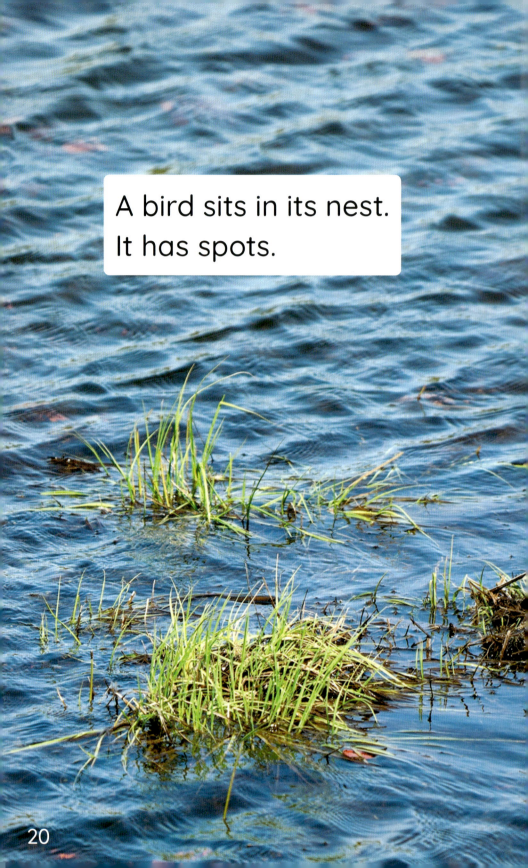

A bird sits in its nest. It has spots.

Lots of animals have spots.
Animals have lots of kinds of spots.

More Ideas:

Phonemic Awareness Activity

Practicing S-Blends:
Tell readers they will segment the sounds of story words containing s-blends. Say an s-blend word for readers to segment the sounds. They will slowly stretch out the sounds of each word, tapping the table as they produce each sound. Call attention to where each s-blend is found in each word.

Suggested words:
- slip
- spot
- slop
- past

Extended Learning Activity

Spotting the Spots:
Many animals have spots. Show readers pictures of spotted animals. Ask them what they notice about the spots. Are the spots big or small? What colors are they? Ask readers how the spotted animals are similar to each other. How are they different? Challenge readers to write a short description of a spotted animal using a few words with s-blends.

Published by Picture Window Books, an imprint of Capstone.
1710 Roe Crest Drive, North Mankato, Minnesota 56003
capstonepub.com

Copyright © 2026 by Capstone.
All rights reserved. No part of this publication may be reproduced in whole or in part, or stored in a retrieval system, or transmitted in any form or by any means, electronic, mechanical, photocopying, recording, or otherwise, without written permission of the publisher.

Library of Congress Cataloging-in-Publication Data is available on the Library of Congress website.

ISBN: 9798875227004 (hardback)
ISBN: 9798875229800 (paperback)
ISBN: 9798875229787 (eBook PDF)

Image Credits: iStock: Ally E, 8, davit85, 15; Shutterstock: acceptphoto, 14, Alex Zotov, 4-5, Aline Bedard, 20-21, Bob Pool, 10-11, Dirk Ercken, 17, Dominik freelancer, 24, EcoPrint, 19, Henk Bogaard, 22-23, JackDiver, 6-7, John A. Anderson, 9, Joshua Trigg, 16, ShutterGlow, 1, 12-13, Uzo Borewicz, 18, Vaganundo_Che, cover, WildSidePhotography, 2-3